Treasures in the Sea

By Robert M. McClung

Books for Young Explorers

NATIONAL GEOGRAPHIC SOCIETY

**B**ugles blare as sailors load supplies aboard their ships and get ready to go to sea. They haul up the huge anchors and set the sails. A gun booms on one of the big ships to let everyone know it is time to leave. Flags wave in the breeze.

A fleet of Spanish ships, carrying gold and silver, is ready to sail for home far across the sea. The time is a hot July day, long, long ago. The place is the harbor of Havana, in Cuba.

Slowly the ships begin to move. One after the other they glide past the great fort guarding the harbor. The wide ocean lies ahead.

Several days later the ships begin to roll and pitch in rough seas off the coast of Florida. The fleet is running into a storm.

The sky grows dark as night and strong winds rip the sails. Giant waves crash across the decks. The ships toss about like chips of wood as the storm grows worse.

Masts of the ships break, and the torn sails whip in the wind like ribbons. One after another the helpless ships break up and sink. Most of the sailors go down with their ships. But some men reach the shore safely.

One of the ships, with big holes in her side, rests on the bottom of the sea not far from land. Fish swim back and forth where the treasure lies — the pieces of eight, the gold coins, the heavy bars of silver.

Soon afterward, the Spanish send divers to try to recover some of the lost treasure.

The divers carry large stones to help them sink quickly. They hold their breath and go down to the sunken ship. They find part of the treasure and begin to bring it up. Spanish soldiers on the nearby beach guard the gold and silver.

 **B**ut pirates hear about the lost treasure, too. They attack the Spaniards and take the gold and silver.

In those days many pirates roamed the seas looking for ships to rob. Swarming aboard, they captured the crews and passengers, and then took what they wanted from the ships.

One of the boldest pirates was Blackbeard. He had a long black beard which he braided and often tied with ribbons. When he attacked a ship, he stuck long, burning matches into his hair. Sometimes it seemed to be on fire.

 **B**lackbeard was
a giant of a man.
When he led
his pirate crew
on a raid, he
carried a big

swordin one hand and a pistol
in the other.

Waving his sword and gun, he
would jump aboard the ship and
roar at the top of his lungs.
Many of Blackbeard's victims
probably were so frightened
that they gave up without a fight.

After a raid, Blackbeard would
sail away to some deserted place.
There he and his crew sometimes
buried their treasure to hide it.

The pirates sailed under a flag
with a skull and crossbones on it.
It was called the Jolly Roger.

Blackbeard and pirates like him disappeared a long time ago. But much of the gold and silver they fought over still lies in sunken ships on the bottom of the sea. Treasure hunters often find the lost ships by looking at old charts that show places where the ships went down.

Once a wrecked ship is found, the treasure hunter dives down to it. He wears an Aqua-Lung, which lets him breathe underwater.

The diver feels light as a feather. Above him, the sun shimmers down through the water.

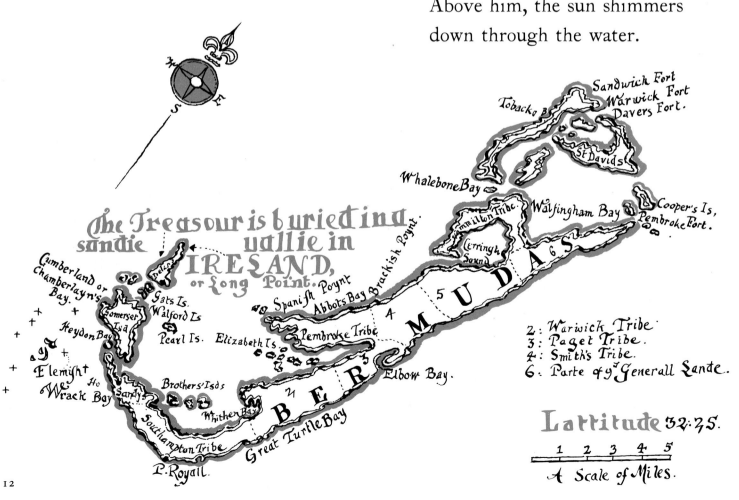

The Treasour is buried in a sandie vallie in IRELAND, or Long Point.

Cumberland or Chamberlayn's Bay.
Gats Is.
Walford Is.
Somerset Isd
Heydon Bay
Pearl Is.
Heymist
Wrack Bay
Elizabeth Is.
Sandy.
Brothers' Isds
Whithen Bay
Southampton Tribe
Great Turtle Bay
P. Royall.
Spanish Poynt
Abbots Bay
Brackish Poynt.
Pembroke Tribe
Elbow Bay.

Tobacko B.
Sandwick Fort
Warwick Fort
Davers Fort.
St Davids
Whalebone Bay
Walsingham Bay
Hamilton Tribe
Cooper's Is.
Pembroke Fort.
Harringt Sound

B E R M U D A S

2: Warwick Tribe.
3: Paget Tribe.
4: Smith's Tribe.
6: Parte of ye Generall Lande.

Lattitude 32:25.

| 1 | 2 | 3 | 4 | 5 |

A Scale of Miles.

The treasure hunter swims past strange animals that look like flowers. They are called sea anemones. On the bottom just ahead he spots the wreckage of an old sailing ship.

Other divers swim down to join the treasure hunt. They all start to explore the sunken ship. First they place plastic pipes above the wreckage to divide it into squares. The divers search the squares one by one. In this way they can be sure that they check every part of the ship carefully.

They find an old cannon covered with coral, and a rusted anchor. Then someone sees a gleam of gold and picks up a coin almost hidden in the sand. He spots another coin—and another!

A fter searching for gold and silver and jewels, the undersea hunters may gather pottery and tools and many other things from old wrecks. These are treasures of the sea, too. They show how people lived long ago.

A diver finds a huge jug, and sends it to the surface.

Another diver fastens a chain about the old cannon. Then he watches as it is hauled up.

After the jug and cannon have been cleaned, they will be sent to a museum where visitors can see them and learn about the past.

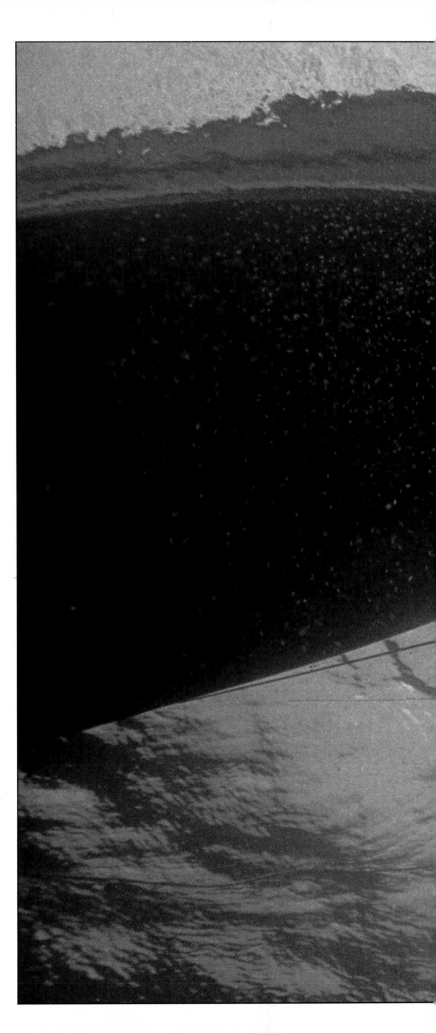

Searching near a huge anchor from an old ship, a treasure hunter picks up a bottle made a long time ago. Just beyond the bottle, he sees some ornaments almost covered by the sand.

Divers find valuable jewelry, too. There is a gold cross with rich green gems. Beside the cross is a gold earring with a face on it. One ornament is shaped like a fish with a curly tail. Nearby is a little golden figure, and a small gold medal. A Spanish knight might have worn the medal many years ago. Perhaps it was part of a pirate's treasure lost in a storm at sea.

The treasure hunters get very excited as they find more and more precious objects. Divers clear sand away from the bottom of the ocean and uncover heavy bars of silver. There are many gold and silver coins, too.

The gold coins that have been covered by the sand shine like new. The salty sea water has made the silver coins turn green over the years.

The coins have many shapes and sizes. A few of them come from countries in Europe. But most of them are stamped with marks that show they were made in America by the Spanish long ago. Some have faces of kings on them. One shows a man with a bushy beard.

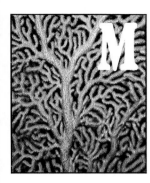M any divers find the creatures of the sea more beautiful than jewels or coins. They watch the undersea life all about them. They see fish darting past, sponges, lacy sea fans, and rainbow-colored corals.

A school of fat golden fish, brighter than any coin, swims around one of the divers. Their shiny scales flash like showers of sparks in the dark waters. These fish are treasures, too.

The fish are not frightened by the divers. They are interested in the big strangers. Sometimes the divers even carry food with them to give to the fish.

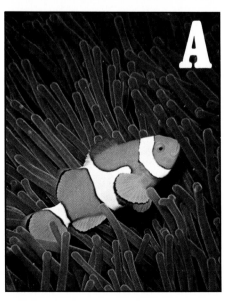

A school of fish with glittering silver sides drifts past. Then others swim slowly into view. They seem to glow like fireflies on a summer night.

Fins waving, a tiny orange and white clownfish darts out to inspect the diver. Suddenly, a big red fish with white polka dots comes out of a dark cave in the coral.

As they watch the natural beauties of the sea, divers must always be on the lookout for danger. There are jellyfish that might sting them, and sharp coral. Fish called barracuda have razor-sharp teeth.

Big sharks sometimes come to circle the divers and watch them with unblinking eyes. The sharks don't often attack them, but the divers can never be sure!

If a giant octopus seized a diver with its eight thick arms, it could keep him from getting back to the surface. But the octopus is shy, and hardly ever attacks. It shoots out a cloud of inky fluid to hide behind and quickly swims away from any danger.

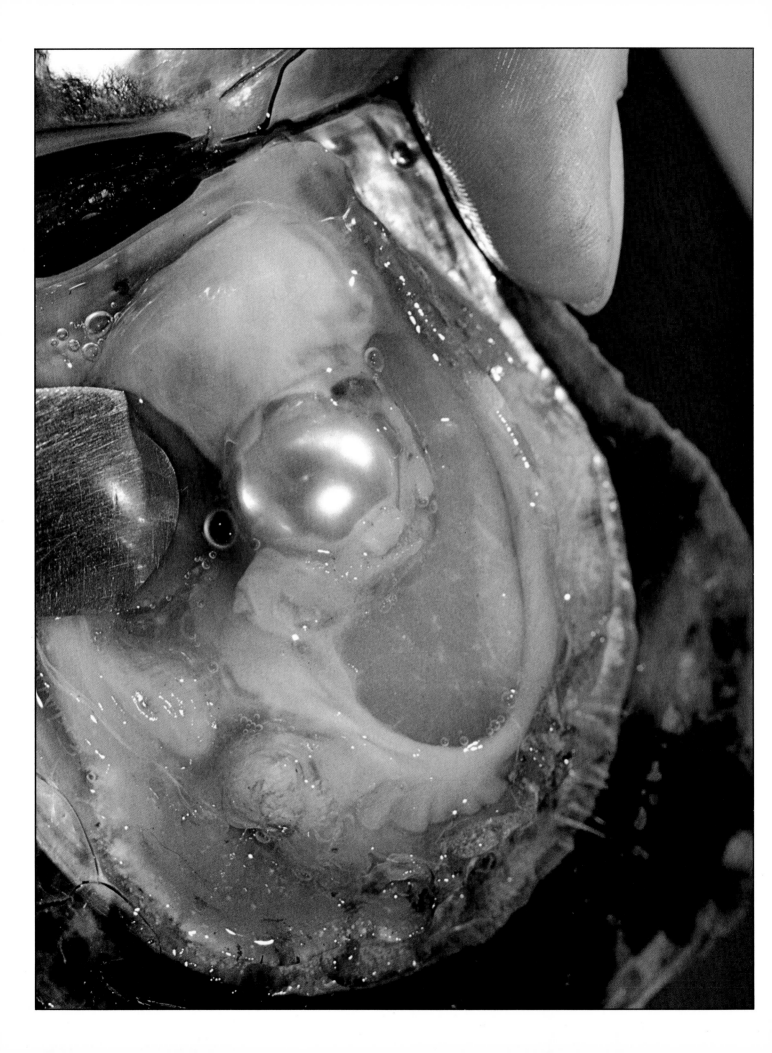

**D**ivers risk all the dangers of the sea to gather pearl oysters. A pearl is one of the sea's most beautiful treasures. It is formed inside the oyster's shell.

Seashells are colorful and beautiful, too. Many people collect them. The best time to look for shells is after a storm, when waves often wash them

up on the beach. Some seashells are rare and valuable.

The people on many Pacific islands have used shells as money

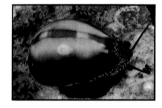

and jewelry. American Indians once made purple and white beads from the shells of clams. They used them in ceremonies and for trading with other tribes.

The sea is always changing. Some days it is stormy, other days peaceful. Sometimes it is rough, sometimes playful. It sparkles in the path of the rising sun and gleams like silver in the light of the moon. Below its surface lies a strange, beautiful world.

Today there are parks under the sea.
Divers can swim in them along
underwater trails with signs
to show the way. No living things
can be harmed here. Visitors can see
forests of coral, brightly colored fish,
beautiful waving sea fans, and shells.
All of these are treasures of the sea.

Prepared by the Special Publications Division of the National Geographic Society
Melvin M. Payne, President; Melville Bell Grosvenor, Editor-in-Chief; Gilbert M. Grosvenor, Editor.

Illustrations Credits